THINK WITH LOVE

A Simple Choice for a Better Life

THINK WITH LOVE: A Simple Choice for a Better Life
By Adriana Cascata
Copyright © 2013 Adriana Cascata.

Published by ROYAL BLUE HOUSE
P. O. Box 723 - Bedford Hills, NY 10507 – U.S.A.

ISBN: 978-0-9854320-2-7
Library of Congress Control Number: 2013917686
Printed in the United States of America

THINK WITH LOVE

A Simple Choice for a Better Life

ADRIANA CASCATA

ACKNOWLEDGEMENTS

This book would not have been written if I had not chosen to think about the meaning of Love. I am in debt to all my companions in this adventure we call life; I could not possibly thank all by name. Therefore, I will mention only some of them here. My husband, Eduardo Iannici, who encouraged me to write this book. Thank you for reading the text; your positive comments helped me tremendously. Thank you to my daughter, Carla, who gives me her unconditional love, and teaches me something different every day. I am particularly grateful to Dr. Edgardo A. López, a brilliant physician with a unique humane approach to the healing process. My special thanks to Pilar Biondi, for her friendship and support. Finally, I deeply appreciate the superb quality of the editing of this book; Leslie O'Brien's precise imprint is on each paragraph.

CONTENTS

MY STORY

I remember the day I started thinking about the meaning of life. I was eight years old and my grandfather was sick with cancer. Given that research was still so underdeveloped, doctors in the 1970s were not yet very optimistic about recovery. I remember asking my mother if my grandfather was going to die. "I do not know," she answered. I asked again, "What happens to us when we pass away?" My mother, with her understanding at that moment, said, "Nothing happens...you die, then you are buried in a coffin underground and worms eat you." This answer triggered my life search for the truth about our existence.

Today, I understand that my mother's answer about death was based on a physical point of view, as it referred only to the body. That answer, while limited, bothered me... so I was determined to look for the true meaning of life, and not only the transition of our physical existence. What is life? What is death? If we are merely a body, nothing in life makes sense. Some people still believe that life finishes once our body decomposes. If so, what about our present life? What about the person I am today? Where is this person going? What about the people I love? Thinking only in physical terms, our life becomes meaningless.

During my teens, I started reading metaphysical books, literature about the hidden universe, the world that we cannot see, but feel and experience every day. I became interested in philosophy and everything related to the study of the mind; however, I did not start my formal studies in psychology until I reached my thirties. The study of human behavior fascinated me, but I kept telling myself, "All these psychological concepts are great but this table is missing a leg." There must be something that keeps all these components together. After many years of logical thinking, introspection and investigation, I realized that there is a spiritual dimension that makes our physical life worthwhile. Love is the essence of that spiritual dimension and the power of our own thought is the key to connecting with that Source. After many different experiences, I know that the way we think is the most important ingredient in our life. The kind of event that you are going through is less important. What matters are the kinds of thoughts that accompany that experience. Think with Love and you will discover the immensity of your entire Life within yourself! Think with Love to build a meaningful life!

Adriana Cascata

INTRODUCTION

What is This Book About?

This book is about you.

My aim is that you feel better after reading it. It's a very simple goal, if you are willing to consider the ideas presented in the following pages.

Each chapter will flow as follows. First, I will formulate the problem, then the main goal, and finally, give you a solution based on very simple, but powerful ingredients.

Let's start!

The Problem

Do you feel...

- Nervous?

- Doubtful, fearful, worried, confused?

- Dissatisfied with your body?

- Sick or weak?

- Life is unfair?

- Depressed?

- People do not understand you?

- You cannot get rid of conflicting relationships?

The Goal

You can feel...

- Calm.

- Confident, safe, faithful, enlightened.

- Satisfied with your body.

- Healthy, strong.

- Everything happens for a reason.

- United with nature and with everyone.

- You can have effortless communication with every person.

- You can have harmonious, productive relationships.

As you can see, the good news is that there is another way to perceive your experiences. Our physical life is based on our senses and we normally believe only what those senses capture. However, there is another world beyond our senses. You can learn how to grasp that world to overcome challenges, handle conflicts and live healthy with abundance and inner peace.

What is the Solution?

The solution is to think with Love.

Love is a Universal principle and an energizing force, which can be visible by loving yourself, others and animals, as well as all of nature.

Where Does All This Lead Me?

To be the first to find Love, inside of you. There is a place within you where the strength of Love abides. You need to be willing to become aware of it and then you will see Love everywhere!

When you think and decide with Love, all decisions become as easy and as right as breathing.

What Do I Have to Do?

You need to conceive another way of thinking strongly and permanently.

Keep the thought of Love in your mind at all times. It changes your life, enriches your experiences and gives you a sense of higher purpose in your life. That new vision will make you a happy person.

How Can I Do That?

You can achieve this by practicing the principles you will find here in this book. Choose another way of thinking about yourself, about other people, and the world. Like a natural consequence of that process, you will fulfill a better way of living.

When Do I Have to Practice?

You need to educate yourself to think with Love during every moment of your life. I invite you to become fully aware that this method works. This requires no effort on your part, but you need to be willing to put these ideas into practice.

What is the Advantage?

Thinking with Love sets you free. If you feel free, you are able to accomplish whatever goals you set your mind to do.

How Long Does it Take to Learn?

You can find out how to think with Love now, as you continue reading this book, and get quick results. However, it is a life-long learning process that will improve the quality of your life.

◆◆◆

Why is Love so Important?

Love is important because only someone who thinks with Love is capable of experiencing it and, like a natural consequence, expressing it.

It is only through the experience of this emotion that you are able to achieve an integration of your mind, body and soul in order to be happy.

Bigger Picture

Think for a moment about the world we live in. Does it satisfy you all the time? Not always, right? Did you think why? The answer is simple: Because you are thinking in a limited way.

Do I Really Think in a Limited Way?

Yes, nearly everyone does. Since our childhood, we learned to think fragmentally. We consider every component of a situation separately and most of the time we are incapable of finding an integrated solution.

Is There a Better Direction We can Take?

Of course! When you perceive a situation, you need to bring all the pieces together in order to be able to understand how the Universe works.

What is Love?

Love is the motor of the Universe.

Love is the Source.

Love is the Light.

All things are made of Love.

Love is where we come from.

Love is a healing power.

Love is the force that keeps everything together.

◆ ◆ ◆

How Can I Grasp Love?

You can grasp Love by using your intelligence and opening your heart, allowing you to discover a world beyond your physical senses.

People think that there are different ways to live and enjoy life, but the only way to be truly happy is through Love.

The Power of Love

The power of Love is in you and it is a great spiritual power that you have at your disposal. Love can be dormant or active within you, according to the way you think.

How Does *The Power of Love* Work?

Consider yourself a body that has to be satisfied with food, sex, money, careers and status. This is a very limited vision of your life. You need to elevate your sight in order to have a vision of the Whole, a Spiritual Vision.

What if I am not a Spiritual Person?

We are all spiritual beings. The spiritual realm is a dimension beyond the physical one.

Without denying or neglecting your physical state, you are able to raise the level of your thinking to experience the Love you are.

You are Love

This book is a reminder of your true essence. You are Love. We all are made of Love. If you accept this fact, your life will change forever. For the better.

Can I be Happy Thinking with Love?

Absolutely! If you live your life with Love, you perceive the world and your relationships differently. You realize that happiness is possible, no matter what happens around you.

The only requirement is your willingness to accept Love consciously. Your will is a dynamic soul force that needs to be activated.

The Great Spiritual Power

As a human being, your own thinking is a great resource and is a power you were born with.

The fact that you are reading this book now, your life, relationships, jobs, as well as everything that has happened to you up until this point, are a result of your own thinking.

Why are my Thoughts so Important?

They are important because your thoughts are the bricks that built your life and the bridge that connects you with others.

Connection of Love's Energy

Love is an energy that flows in the air; you cannot see it but you can feel it.

Thinking in a loving way about someone produces a real connection with this person.

Solving Problems

We all face obstacles in our life and if you choose to think with Love, you will not quarrel anymore, but seek real solutions.

Instead, you will overcome any obstacle by understanding the entire situation in order to find the best result.

Do I Need a Teacher?

A teacher can help you during your first few steps but ultimately the experience is all yours. The Greater Teacher is a part of you.

Seek and Find

Try to reach that place within you where the activity of the mind ceases, and where you feel Love.

Some people are embarrassed by the idea of Love. Is that your case? You may ask for help inside yourself, and a voice within you will answer.

Your Inner Voice

Your inner voice is the link within your true essence, Love. You can call it your inner guide, intuition, etc. The name is not important; its function is what is significant. You sometimes hear this voice but you forget to consult it.

A New You

Everything is experience! When Love is reached at a conscious level, whatever happens in your life has a solution, however serious the situation may seem.

Discover the connection that leads you to Love and your life will change forever.

◆ ◆ ◆

Love is *Your* Source

We all come from the same Source, so you cannot live apart from Love. The reason that you think you can is your extreme identification with your body.

Is my Body the Problem?

No, your body is not the problem. The problem is the extreme identification with it. How we view our bodies and our identification with it strengthens our perception of separation.

I have my body, you have yours and therefore we are two human beings, entirely different and separate from each other. Each one of us has an identity with which we classify ourselves and which others can recognize.

At a physical level, this is completely true but the story does not end there.

◆ ◆ ◆

Willingness to Change

We live in a body, but we are much more than a physical entity. You must realize that the true cause of your separation lies in the beliefs you hold in your mind.

We are too attached to our thinking, as such we have to start with the first step: Willingness to change.

Real Challenge

Your current difficulties in life and the solutions to them are only tiny pieces of this enormous puzzle. Because you are thinking in a limited way, you have to accept that the better solution may be different from what you initially thought. That is a big challenge for most of us.

Miracle of Thinking

Everything you desire, from the simplest thing to the most sophisticated one starts with a thought. Learn how to think in the right way: with Love.

Thinking is the miraculous function of the mind. Your goal is to educate your mind to think in a certain way in order to have a meaningful life.

The Trained Swimmer

Think with Love in every situation and you will always be able to find the best outcome.

It requires practice, such as swimming in a vast ocean. A trained swimmer would tell you that it is a very pleasant experience. However, it requires training, perseverance, patience and flexibility to overcome unexpected obstacles.

◆◆◆

Getting Results

As long as you learn this new way of thinking, you will incorporate a new vision into your life and you will be fascinated by how everything changes for you.

Evolution of Thinking

Use your thoughts to improve your life. You now know that everything that occurs has the ability to unfold the Love that you are.

Love is the Infinite Mind

Love is where we come from, the Infinite Mind. In fact, it makes little difference what name we give it. What matters is connecting with this Love and living in its consciousness.

Think about it in the way you prefer: You can imagine Love as Light, a Supreme Intelligence, Abundance, Peace, Health and/or Harmony.

Where Can I Find that Love?

Love is in your mind and in your heart.

Love is in other people's minds and hearts.

We can find Love in nature; with its trees and flowers and all the miraculous products we can reap from it.

Our pets are an expression of Love.

Love is a powerful Presence that lies within you and around us right now. It joins Heaven and Earth.

Believe it or Not

Believing in the reality of Love is your choice. You will realize that these ideas are true. If you believe in Love, your journey in life will be easier.

Benefits of Thinking with Love

• A new perception: You gain a new vision about yourself, your relationships and about life.

• You can work at your own pace: You go through the process of thinking with Love according to your needs.

• Freedom: You discover that you are free to choose what to believe, what to think and what decisions to make.

• Wellness: You experience wellness as a result of an integration of your mind, body and soul.

• Awareness: You increase your sense of responsibility as a human being.

◆ ◆ ◆

PART ONE

MIND, BODY AND SOUL

CHAPTER 1

MIND

You are a Mental Being

Everything that happens in your life starts in your mind. When you have a problem to solve, you have to be able to perceive your dilemma as a part of the whole.

A Container

Think of your mind as a container where water flows permanently. That circulation of water represents the dynamics of your own thoughts, and they are coming from two different sources: The Great Ocean and little watercourses.

The Majestic Ocean

That energy of water represents thoughts that you think using your Source, the Great Ocean of Love, within yourself. It brings an unlimited calm and continuous course of water that flows through you and back to the Ocean again, where all of us belong.

The other stream of water comes from outside yourself; this energy stands for the thoughts you have as a result of your perception of the world you live in.

However, your false beliefs give these watercourses the power to produce tsunamis and high waves, breaking everything that comes in contact with them.

Control your Thoughts

Very few people understand the real power of the mind. Nobody remains fully aware of it all the time. This is usually because there are many things we have to do in our ordinary life, so it seems difficult for all of us to engage in constant thought watching. However, if you want to rid yourself of worries and fear, you need to control your thoughts.

Within your Self *is* the Power

Each day, each hour, each minute, each second, you are thinking. The power of thinking is all yours.

The most powerful stream of energy comes from inside yourself and it is connected with the Love that you are.

Powerful Creator

You are the only one who makes decisions in your mind, nobody else.

Your mind is very powerful; it is always creating and in no way loses its creative force. It never sleeps (even if your body is resting), and it is working according to your thinking.

Make your Choice

Your physical experience makes you perceive a limited world. You need to educate your mind to believe in what you cannot see. It is your own choice.

Does the Mind Grow?

The purpose of all life is development. Everything living has a sense of growth. Your mind is no exception and it develops its capacity through the power of your thoughts.

Meaningful World

I propose a simple task. First, think with Love about yourself. Next, think with Love about every living creature in every circumstance. This is the only chance you have to find a meaningful world.

◆ ◆ ◆

Be Responsible

Do not leave your mind unguarded!

It is your responsibility to choose what content you hold in your mind. It is up to you to control your thoughts.

Positive and Negative Thoughts

Your thoughts create your life.

We can distinguish two different kinds of thoughts: Positive and negatives ones.

Both circulate through your mind although they come from different sources.

When you have positive thoughts, you are allowing the stream of water from yourself to flow freely. The result is peace and happiness.

Conversely, negative thoughts make you believe that the watercourse flowing from outside yourself has power. The result of that false belief is conflict and sadness.

Neutral Thoughts

In our world of polarities, neutral thoughts do not exist. Every thought has the power to create a good or bad experience.

Think only Positive Thoughts

Every time you have a problem, if you focus your attention on it, you increase both your fear and the problem. Instead, think only positive thoughts. Eventually, those fears will be replaced with solutions.

Positive thoughts about you and others are a clear manifestation of Love.

Letting Go of Fear

Self-education is essential to align your thoughts with the Love within you and rid yourself of fear.

Attitude is Everything

The power to solve problems and be happy depends upon your attitude and openness to change.

Simple Process

Changing the way you think is a simple process. However, it requires your willingness, work and patience.

Willingness to change opens the door to miracles.

Working to educate your mind helps you achieve your goals.

Patience keeps you calm until the results come.

Nature

Think for a moment about nature and observe things beyond your senses; you will find that nature is simply a physical manifestation of Love.

Animals, for example, have Love for their own offspring and they find the need to protect them because they regard them as a part of themselves.

Looking Beyond your Senses

Our physical nature (one who seeks food, shelter, sex, money) is the only one that responds to material stimuli. However, there is a real energy beyond our eyes. You need to learn that new Universe in order to experience inner peace.

◆ ◆ ◆

Climb out of your Capsule

The reason why you may be embarrassed by Love is due to fear. This false idea about life keeps you encapsulated. It is time to step out of the box.

Despite what your physical eyes see, this world we live in is full of Love.

Think with Love and you will be the first to find yourself surrounded by it every day.

Vision of Love

Love is the greatest energy at your disposal. Recognize that power within yourself to see it in the outside world. It is a maturation process that works from the inside out. When you are ready, you will bring it into your life naturally.

Mind your Own Business

If you become heavily involved with these ideas, you may try to convince others. Mind your own business and do not interfere with other people's process.

Others might misunderstand your offer of help as overly pushy, generating negative effects for both of you.

When someone is ready, he or she will go in search of answers; only at that time will your guidance be helpful to that person.

Resistance

Our struggle to overcome our resistance to change the way we think is enormous!

The adjustment can be challenging because your old patterns and beliefs want to prevail. Do not be afraid and do it.

Two Basic Emotions

From the time you wake up in the morning until you go to bed, every external stimulus you perceive, what you read, every news you listen to and what you think about generates in you a positive emotion like Love or a negative one like fear. Everything comes from what you believe and what you think.

Love and fear are the result of your own thinking.

Choose to think with Love to have a good life for yourself and for those around you.

Unity of Love

We are here to remember that we are Love. Love is our common Source so we are all united at that level of the mind.

Thoughts of Love or union link you with other people. Perceiving others beyond the body helps you understand real life.

Real Communication

Imagine thoughts as if they are a breeze.

Every time you think about your friend that lives thousands of miles away, you are communicating with that person. You send them a little breeze and the other person is capable of feeling it.

If you have the chance to hug your friend, that is great! Yet the relevant encounter between two people is through their thoughts. If you charge your thoughts with Love, that blessing reaches both of you.

Sharing Love

Remember that in the depths of each person's heart, there is Love, no matter how frivolous people can be or how materialistic they may seem. Some people have this Light on the surface and others in the depths of their soul. Nevertheless, the Light is always there, because Love is always there.

That Light produces an attraction to people who vibrate at the same frequency. Conversely, there can be a strong rejection between people with very different vibrations. That is why we sometimes feel, without apparent reason, an attraction or a rejection to people we do not even know.

Awareness Process

During your childhood, your consciousness is limited. You have to learn everything so you use your mind. Your parents and teachers teach you how to talk, how to eat, how to dress, how to read and write, and even how to pray; but in their own way.

As a child, you still have a strong feeling of separation from everyone, and the world; you are not conscious of the Love within you yet. You think that you are unique, and your wants and needs are what's important.

During your youth, you are busy building the world outside you by studying, going to college, working, traveling and so on. Later on, you are busy raising a family, buying a house and doing everything that is expected of you.

Mental Adulthood

Hopefully, one day, you realize that beyond your physical world of wants and needs something is missing... that is the time to start your conscious journey of Love.

From this point, you are a new person because you are developing the pathway to Love within yourself. You start thinking in a better way, which will change your overall behavior in life.

Journey to Love

Carefully choosing what you think is the first step down this path.

This new milestone in your life will allow you to harmonize and integrate your mind, body and soul in all your material achievements and goals. This integration will give you a new vision.

Synthesis

Science evolves giving us more information about the world than ever before. As such, there are new paradigms that help us see things in a different way now.

Thinking with Love is the synthesis to solving any problem in your life. Why? Because by doing so, it brings the Intelligence of the Universe into your heart.

Making Decisions

You can change your life the moment you make the decision to do so. Decisions begin based on the way we think and how we think is conditioned by our beliefs.

The Believer

A belief is something that you hold in your mind because you think it is true. All beliefs are real to the believer. Most of our beliefs come from our upbringing and are not well grounded.

Do I Have to Change my Beliefs?

At the very least, you have to examine them. The best way to protect your beliefs is not to consider them.

Whatever you believe, it is true for you. Your beliefs have an extraordinary power, and none of them is neutral. You have the power to dictate each decision you make based on those beliefs.

Generally speaking, we are not used to reviewing our beliefs out of fear. If you start thinking with Love now, that process will help you to be open-minded. You will realize that there is nothing to fear.

Hands-on

When everything goes smoothly in your life, there is nothing to worry about. But, when something is not working properly, it is time for a review. If you realize that a belief is interfering with the solution to a problem, it is time to change it. Replace that old belief with a new one,

one that you think will lead you to the best outcome.

Worthwhile Training

Educate your mind to think with Love and in time, you will do it automatically.

You are capable of doing it because it is your natural condition.

Our parents, teachers and mentors guide us to fulfill our goals, but few of them remark on the importance of loving thoughts for our own benefit.

True Education

During your training process, you will need to teach your mind to replace unproductive thoughts with useful ones.

Every time a negative thought pops up in your mind, turn your attention away from it immediately, replacing it with a positive one.

Thought Replacement

Your negative thoughts keep you away from your goals. The only way to get rid of a destructive thought is to replace it immediately with a constructive one. You cannot reject it directly.

A Great Habit

Get into the habit of optimistic thinking to achieve your goals. As soon as any thought of disharmony, illness or scarcity crosses your mind, replace it immediately, thinking of harmony, health and abundance.
The mind does not recognize what is true or false. The mind is a container of water that depends on you to open one valve or the other.

What you think, you bring into your life.

Practice, Practice, Practice

It is essential to practice this new way of thinking on a daily basis. Like learning a new language or sport, you need to practice to see results.

Thoughts gain strength through repetition. Here are some thoughts that you can work with every day.

- I am Love.

- Today, I see only Love.

- I am willing to discover Love, here.

Sometimes, a situation breaks down in a way where you are unable to see Love in it. There is always Love, even behind the most catastrophic circumstances.

Place Within Your Self

Think positively and try to reach that deep place within yourself.

When a person or a situation comes to your mind, think positively.

If you feel that a person has damaged you in any way, try to understand that person. Try to see him or her from a different perspective and with compassion, thinking, "Oh boy, you need Love, because you must feel its lack of it for you to behave that way." Then, bless this person.

You can send a loving thought even in the most negative situation.

Love is an Extension

Think with Love toward every person, creature or situation and always wish him or her, the best. It works! And not only for the other person. Because by doing so, you increase the consciousness of Love within yourself too.

Give Love and you will extend it.

Practice this simple thought today and soon you will reap the positive results. It is so simple and so powerful!

Every time you face a challenging experience with others, stay calm and serene. Remember that any inadequate behavior from someone is his or her fear or problem. Not yours. I practice this all the time and I assure you that it works. The results will convince you.

Cause and Effect

Love is the Cause. We are the Effect. This Universal Law applies every day of your life, through your thoughts and actions.

What you think toward others (good or bad) comes back to you.
Bless everything you see. That blessing will come back to you (multiplied), because that is the Law of Cause and Effect.

Moving On

If you are stuck, angry or resentful about something that happened to you, change your mind. Now you realize that those emotions hurt you and are the result of an old thought pattern. Replace them with a loving thought.

Move on!

◆ ◆ ◆

Good News

The good news is that changing depends on you. Yes, it is up to you to change your thoughts; it is your decision.

Be watchful with your thoughts. Are you thinking a constructive thought right now? If so, you are on the right path to learning. If not, you need to change.

Thinking always produces effects in your life. Right thinking brings positive outcomes; wrong thinking leads to bad ones.

Your Thoughts Shape your Character

Your character arises from your thought habits. Think constructively and you will build yourself a strong character. You cannot think loving thoughts and be unkind at the same time.

Your Thoughts Modify Everything

Your health and your environment are affected by your thinking. If your life is not working, change your thinking to modify those conditions.

When you want to change your outer conditions, the first thing you have to do is change your thoughts. If you are not happy in the city you live in, the first thing you should do is start thinking about moving. You can apply the same attitude to your job or any relationship.

Start right now!

Keep a Positive Mental Attitude

Everything you accomplish in your domestic life, businesses and relationships are affected by your mental attitude.

Every thought brings some kind of result.

If you perceive disharmony at any level, recognize that it is only a result of letting yourself think in a manner contrary to Love.

Faith Increases Good Results

Your willingness to think with Love brings you new results and increases your faith.

Having confidence in these Universal Principles is what gives you the opportunity to realize that they work.

Great thoughts without faith create no results.

Put all your faith in the eternal, changeless and forever unfailing Love that abides within you and you will experience miracles in your life.

❖ ❖ ❖

Thoughts to Steer by

1.   You are a mental being.

2.   Control your thoughts.

3.   Your mind is a powerful Creator.

4.   Think only positive thoughts.

5.   Overcome resistances.

6.   Real communication is through the mind.

7.   Examine your beliefs.

8.   Apply thought replacement.

9.   Practice, practice, practice.

10. Your thoughts modify everything.

CHAPTER 2

BODY

Integrated Universe

Perceiving yourself only as a physical body reinforces your belief in separation.

Obviously, you reside in a body because you are living in a physical world. Your body is a living organism composed of cells, tissues and organs. It is limited in time and space and driven by biochemical processes such as the respiratory, digestive and circulatory systems. But your body is part of an integrated Universe that works as a Whole.

Your Biggest Fear

Our identification with our body is enormous. Think for a moment, what is your biggest fear? If you answered this question, you will realize that all your fear is related to your body, such as developing an illness, having an accident, old age, being in debt, losing your job or your home, etc.

Thinking with Love lets you get rid of the fear associated with your body.

Socializing Device

You are a spiritual being passing through a physical experience. The bodily organism where you are living now is the shelter of your soul, as well as a unique communication device.

It works as a vehicle through which you can operate effectively in this physical plane. While you are here, the actual function of your body is to allow Love to speak to others through you.

Proper Communication

While the unity at the body level is a form of contact, the only true communication occurs at the level of the mind.

Bodily Needs

Like all biological beings, our mind regulates our body. Contrary to what we believe, our needs are the result of our thoughts.

The Traveler

Birth and death are not the beginning or the end. Life is a continuum. Your soul is a traveler and the body you have now is the perfect transportation device for it.

There is a belief in death based on a physical perception. Believing in the reality of death is to have a very limited view about the evolution of the human race.

Four Seasons

After fulfilling their life cycle, leaves fall off the branches and drop. Like the trees, our life continues its journey throughout this physical process.

Even though it is sad when someone we love dies, we must learn to think of death in the same way.

Death is an important issue that awakened my curiosity when I was a child. I thought that if death was real and one day my parents passed away, I would never be happy again. Now I understand that all human beings have to continue their soul's evolution as a part of life.

Living Forever

When we talk about death, what actually dies is the body. Our soul lives forever.

Death should be a quiet choice, made with joy and a sense of peace. The body has been treated with kindness throughout this journey, which ultimately leads to the Source of Love.

Be grateful to your body for the service it provides you while you are here.

Fragment

The experience of living temporarily in a body is what we call life, but this is only a fragment.

Our souls travel. They pass through from one body to another in order to evolve but we are always connected to the Source of Love, which is where all of us come from.

You reside in a marvelous vehicle that allows your soul to express itself while in this physical dimension. The Love you are, for a little while, must still be expressed from one body to another.

Housekeeping

You have to keep your body in good shape because it is the home for your soul. Taking care of it means keeping your body away from excess of any kind. Maintaining a clear mind and feeding your body healthy food keeps it vigorous and strong.

Physical *and* Spiritual

Looking after your body does not distance you from your spiritual development. On the contrary, it will pave the way for it.

The Key

Your mind and body are connected. You need to achieve a proper integration of the two in order to be healthy. Your thoughts influence your brain and your brain controls the systems in your body.

Be alert to your thoughts. Remember that your mind is the master key to achieving a healthy body.

Listen to Your Body

Think carefully before eating something that can cause you any problems. For example, if you know in advance that certain foods do not support your digestive system, nor agree with the proper functioning of your body, avoid them.

Pay attention to your body. Listen to its signals and avoid harmful activity. By spending time trying to reestablish your health, you are deviating from the original purpose of your mind, which is to experience and share Love.

Thinking of Your Body

Your body is your home for a while and as such requires attention and dedication. Knowing and understanding your physical needs is necessary as it allows you to take care of them responsibly.

You may consider this issue unrelated to your thinking. However, there is a direct correlation. What you think creates positive or negative emotions that have a direct impact on your body.

Maintain a healthy body by thinking positive thoughts about yourself, others and life.

Your Call

If you want to keep your mind focused on the important things, you need to keep your body healthy.

Try to find the right balance. Become aware of your physical needs, without making your body the center of your life.

You are much more than a physical entity. Nevertheless, a healthy, harmonious body may help you remember the true beauty that lies within yourself; the beauty of your soul.

Best Investment

Working only on the external aspects of your life means your work is incomplete. The best investment lies in a true connection within you.

Strengthening your Immune System

Our cells constantly hear our thoughts and amend them. Negative thoughts cause depression and weaken the immune system. Thoughts of Love strengthen it.

Physical Activity

Like your mind, your body needs exercise. A flexible mind maintains a flexible body; a rigid mind carries on a rigid body.

Do physical exercise to awaken the dormant or repressed feelings in your body.

Stretch, get on your bicycle, practice yoga, do Pilates, practice Tai Chi or Qi Gong, play tennis, ride a horse, toss a ball, walk every day. Choose an activity that fits your body, as well as your personality.

Relaxation

A peaceful mind holds a relaxed body.

Relaxation is for the body.

Peace is for the mind.

Learn to be still because the voice of Love is heard in the stillness.

Breathing

Breathing is extremely important because it integrates the mind with the body.

Breathing is a thought in motion.

Learn to breathe deeply. Take generous breaths to clear your mind. Breathing economically is like having a house with several rooms and using only one, to save the others.

Focus your exercise around your breathing. This is essential in order to keep your brain oxygenated and facilitate your connection with yourself. Let the energy of Love breathe through you.

Sleeping

Sleeping is vital. It plays an important role in the immune system, memory, metabolism, the capacity to learn and many other functions.

A great requisite for healthy sleep is to avoid any negative thoughts. Go to bed happy.

Gratitude

Always be grateful for your day (good or bad).

Feeling and expressing gratitude is medicine for the heart.

Simple Process

This book focuses on ways to control your thoughts at the onset, in order to find Love.

That task will be difficult if you experience your body as a burden. If this is the case, change that belief by changing your thinking habits. Think positively about your body!

Good or Bad?

The body is neutral. It is neither good nor bad. It is simply your home for a while.

You do not walk around saying this house is good or this one is bad. We all know that some dwellings are better looking than others are. To make these types of comments about bodies is to respond to certain personal beliefs that have nothing to do with the body's real function.

◆ ◆ ◆

Improve your Body

In order to help relax your body, boost your immune system and enhance your healing process, there are a vast amount of resources that can help us in many ways. Among other programs, you can explore Nutrition Plans, Therapeutic Massage, Cranial Sacral Therapy, Reiki, Reflexology, Aromatherapy and Color Therapy.

Human Sexuality

Sexuality is an instinctive function of human nature that allows for reproduction.

Enjoy your sexuality by being aware of the consequences it can bring, such as unwanted pregnancy or disease. Because of this, sexuality requires responsibility.

Searching for Enlightenment

It is impossible to deny the body. When you hear someone say that the body does not exist, he or she is referring to a metaphysical level. It is not real because it is not eternal, only temporary. Remember that only what is real is forever, like Love and our essence (soul).

The organism we call the body is a process that begins with an embryo, which then transforms into a baby, child, adolescent, adult and elder, until we take our last breath.

Physical death is the process by which the soul detaches from the body.

Health or Disease

The body talks to us; its language is one of health or disease.

Health is the natural state for a human being. A healthy body tells the mind, body and soul to coexist and integrate seamlessly.

When a symptom or disease appears, it is because the mind, body and soul are working in an unbalanced way.

Harmony or Conflict

Disease is the consequence when the mind, body and soul are in conflict.

Health is the result of your mind, body and soul dancing in harmony.

Right Direction

Every time you want to go in one direction and your body wants to go in another, pay attention because this scheme tends to produce great stress.

From now on, every time you feel a minimum discomfort in your body, take the time to think for a moment about what is going on. There is something (thought or behavior) that needs to be changed. Your body always talks to you. Be sure to listen to what it has to say.

Well Being

The body's realization is health. No matter how you feel, every morning as you wake up picture yourself being well, strong and a healthy person.

Looking for Harmony

If your life is comprised of stressful situations, remember that all that stress (on the mental level) is saved on parts of your body with consequences (stomach pain, ulcers, headaches, cancer, etc.).

Stress arises as a conflict between what you really want to do and what you actually do.

Every time you experience any stressful situation, switch your mind and think loving thoughts...

Different Healing Approaches

Besides Allopathic or Homeopathic Medicine, many different approaches are available today to heal you according to your beliefs, choices and budget: Acupuncture, Herbal Medicine, Naturopathic Medicine, Ayurveda, Tibetan Medicine or Traditional Chinese Medicine.

Beyond your treatments, the most imperative factor in your healing process is changing your mind.

If you want to improve your health, clear your thoughts. Look at your illness, your convalescence or your treatment as an opportunity to start thinking with Love.

Working on the Cause

Every conflict between the mind, body and soul has consequences on your body.

If you experience illness, try to find its causes instead of focusing only on the symptoms.

Sometimes it is not easy to determine a cause at a conscious level. Find a therapy according to your preferences and personality.

Forgiveness

Forgive yourself and others. Be willing to dig up the negative energy inside of you to prevent, treat and rid yourself of illness.

Forgiveness is a healing tool.

Forgiveness sets you free.

What should you do in front of a sick person?

Any time you meet someone who is unwell, immediately imagine that person healthy and happy. In your communication, reinforce thoughts of health and union with that person.

That person is experiencing a personal process and he or she has to learn something from that body disorder. You wish that person a speedy recovery and a shorter learning course. Bless this person. Send them only thoughts of Love.

Blessing People

Blessing people is a very positive thought because you are telling this person that he or she is Love.

Remember, this attitude multiplies Love within you.

Thoughts to Steer by

1. The body is a socializing device.

2. Your soul travels through your body.

3. Housekeeping: Avoid excess.

4. Listen to your body.

5. Strengthen your immune system.

6. Physical and spiritual lives are connected.

7. Your choice: Find the right balance.

8. Practice physical activity.

9. Keep your body healthy.

10. Try different kinds of medicine.

CHAPTER 3

SOUL

A Sunray

Think about the sun. Imagine yourself as part of that Source of life. Like a sunray, your soul is part of the Whole.

Your soul is truthfully yourself; that essence is only Love.

Unchanging Soul

Your soul does not change. It does not learn. It is always the same, essence of Love, going through different journeys.

Your soul loves, creates and knows.

Why am I Here?

You are here to share who you are with others, with nature, with animals and with everything on this planet.

Simple Recipe

You gain Love from others only in the proportion that you have it (at a conscious level) within yourself. Does this sound strange? Try it in your daily life and you will be convinced!

New Life

When your soul (spark of Love) incorporates into your body, your life begins. From that moment, you share that energy of Love with everyone and everything.

◆ ◆ ◆

Role Playing

The Universe's Plan is like a big movie representation with a script. Inside of it, you have a specific character to play. Here, on this earth, that particular role is linked to your soul.

Your true potential power lies within you. Discover it and bring it into your life.

Fulfilling your Dreams

You can become or achieve whatever you want by developing your talents. No ability of yours ever stops growing even though it might be hidden for a long time.

Working, studying, improving your skills and directing your thoughts toward Love is the only way to fulfill your dreams. That is the meaning of unfolding your soul.

Unfolding your Soul

Each of us has everything at hand to unfold our soul. The potential resides within us until we decide to release it. To make your decision toward that goal you need to go one-step beyond the visible world.

Big Connection

You, like every other person, has the possibility to connect with your soul. Do it and enjoy the benefits because your soul is always connected with the Source of Knowledge.

Overcoming Obstacles

In order to achieve your goals, you need to remove the blocks that get in the way of the path to your soul.

Those obstacles are your fear. Keep in mind that you can rid yourself of fear by correcting your false beliefs.

What are You Thinking Right Now?

Be aware of what you are thinking!

If you are thinking something that is not positive, stop! Think only positive thoughts! You will feel peace regardless of your circumstances.

Responsibility

As an adult, you are responsible for what you think and how you build your life. No one else has power over you.

Chemical Factor

Scientific research shows that by our thinking, our brain sends information to our body and changes every chemical component of it.

Think with Love to keep your body in balance in order to connect effectively with your soul.

Emotions

Your thinking creates emotions. Any positive or negative thoughts produce feelings of the same level.

Emotions of love, empathy, faith, joy and union, raise your consciousness. A deep level of consciousness connects you with your soul. Conversely, negative emotions keep you away from your true identity.

Learning with Joy

Your present life is a journey through different incarnations. You can consider that journey as different classrooms where you learn lessons.

By thinking with Love, you have the opportunity to pass through every session with the best attitude and learn with joy.

◆ ◆ ◆

Why Joy?

Joy opens the door to your understanding; sadness closes it.

One-step at a Time

You can raise your consciousness by thinking with intelligence beyond your physical senses.

By raising your consciousness, you link yourself with your soul. It is a gradual process that will change your perception of the world.

How Can I Raise my Consciousness?

You raise your consciousness every time you think with Love. You can conceive it by thinking rationally, meditating and/or praying.

What Does it Mean to be Rational?

Rational thinking is the normal way to think. Logical reasoning makes your life possible, improves your environment, solves problems and lets you evolve as a human being.

Logical Outcome

Great scientists discovered a Universe beyond time and space; they arrived there by their rational thinking. That Universe is the world of Love where your soul lives. Love cannot be reached by force; it can only be contacted through your understanding.

Meditation

Meditation disposes of negative thoughts and clarifies your mind. Then confusion vanishes.

There are many techniques to go deeply inside yourself and experience the Love that you are. Find which one fits best for you.

Praying

You can pray in any form you choose. The most important thing is to understand what praying means: Praying is aligning your mind with the Love inside of you.

When you pray you are stepping aside. It is a unique moment of communication between your soul and the Source of Love within you.

Through prayer, Love is received.

Forgiving is Overlooking

Forgiveness is a conscious willingness to be one with the Source of Love, with other people and with nature. When you forgive, you overlook any physical experience. By forgiving, you raise your consciousness from separation to union.

Through forgiveness, Love is expressed.

Next Step

As you transit your spiritual development and become aware of your union with the Source of Love, you start extending your soul. Your talents emerge, and you are on the path to accomplishing your purpose in life.

Matter of Vocation

You need to discover and expand your talents in a harmonious and effective manner. Following your passion and raising your particular talent allows you to shorten your path to Love.

Being Proactive

The natural function of your soul is to manifest its richness with others.

Any expression of art headed in the direction of being meaningful needs to be shared with others. Unfold your soul through your own talents. The result is wellness, joy and a productive life for you and for those around you.

Be Yourself

Everything you have learned is deeply rooted in your mind. Thus, you have to explore if it is productive or not.

Be yourself, and have strength and patience to get over external influences.

Dedicate yourself to do what your heart tells you to do.

Stillness

A simple and practical way to reach your soul is to create a daily habit of sitting down for a little while. Close your eyes and let your thoughts emerge from your mind, like a purification process. After a bit, start thinking about your desires and the things you want to achieve. Try the good and positive experience of a short period of silence. Nothing is more nurturing and refreshing.

Freedom: Main Purpose

Discover your true mental-spiritual dimension by connecting with your soul. That dimension leads you to freedom.

Nobody has power over you, over your beliefs or over your mind. You can build a new life based upon what you think consistently with Love.

Magnet

Your mind projects what you have inside of you.

To change something on the outside, you need to change your mind.

Be vigilant and cultivate only loving thoughts. Once you are willing to do so, your soul acts as a magnet, attracting only the right people into your life.

Think with Love and you will attract Love.

Thoughts to Steer by

1. Connect with your soul.

2. Fulfill your dreams.

3. Overcome obstacles.

4. Take responsibility.

5. Learn with joy.

6. Meditate.

7. Pray.

8. Forgive.

9. Be Yourself.

10. Be a magnet: Think with Love!

PART TWO

LOVE IN ACTION

CHAPTER 4

LOVE IN ACTION

Loving Yourself

You need to love yourself in order to love others.

You need to control your thoughts, take care of your body and connect with your soul. All these activities influence the quality of your relationships.

Mirrors

Your relationships work as a mirror. I am not thinking about perfect rapports (those exist only in the movies), but instead, productive and loving connections.

If you keep inharmonious relationships, you need to clean your mind and as a natural consequence, that person will fade away from your life.

Universal Plan

As part of the Universal Plan and during your journey here, you meet certain people. Some of them you probably like, and others you may dislike. All of them are a part of your relationship map.

From a practical standpoint, you cannot interact with every person on the planet. Therefore, the Universe goes beyond your personal plans and assigns you very specific encounters.

Trusting the Plan

Your relationships are not random chances. In order to learn our reciprocal lessons, those who are destined to meet will meet.

Social Being

Nature is a good example of understanding that every single life form is related to each other in order to evolve.

There is no progress as a human being or any possibility to raise your level of consciousness in isolation from others.

Every one of your relationships has a purpose, even if you do not realize that. You need to find out what you have to learn or to teach from every personal encounter.

You are responsible for any rapport you have undertaken, no matter the reason.

Any problematic liaison is the starting point for forgiveness. Look at it as an opportunity to understand the connection with Love.

Opportunity to Share

The main purpose of your relationships is to share Love. Many of them do not look like that; yet, they are.

Every encounter you have, no matter if it is a moment, a situation, a job, a voyage, or an entire lifetime, is an opportunity to share your true essence of Love.

Same Journey, Different Paths

Think about other human beings as you think about yourself. You will realize that we are all the same. Similar experiences happen to us and everyone else; with different nuances, but craving the same things.

The only difference between people is that we all are traveling different paths. The destination, however, is the same: Love.

Why this Relationship?

The way you think, and the kind of thoughts you hold in your mind build your relationships, they speak about you.

Every one of your relationships begins in your mind. As a consequence, according to the Universal Plan, that particular rapport is a lesson you have to learn.

Different Reactions

Every time we meet people, we have expectations about this encounter and that generates emotions that produce pleasing or unpleasant reactions in our entire body (especially in our heart and in our stomach).

Thinking loving thoughts about everyone helps you feel satisfying results, regardless of the circumstances or the other person.

Three Groups

There are relationships where you share a moment, a certain period of time or a lifetime.

Flash Relationships

You may share a moment with someone you do not even know, for example, when you are in an elevator. This contact is only for a moment. So far, they are still lessons and can evolve into emotions of high intensity but they last for a very short time.

Sharing a Voyage

You also have relationships that last for a certain period, such as a partner, friend, coworker. These contacts involve a commitment and represent more advanced lessons for you to learn.

Lifetime Affairs

Generally referred to parents and children, these interactions are the most difficult to bear because they last your entire life. They require more commitment, understanding and forgiveness than any other relationship.

Love is the Answer

A flash relationship, a voyage or lifetime affairs are lessons on three different levels.

Your task is to think with Love, no matter the relationship level you are involved in.

Focusing on the real meaning of your lessons will make your journey more productive and you will enjoy the process.

Nutritional Issue

Everyone has to deal with complicated interactions throughout life. These situations are part of the journey.

By thinking loving thoughts about people, you will build nutritious relationships. They promote the best in you and in others.

I Prefer...

Feeling preference or experience affinity for certain people is normal. The final goal is to phase out of your mind resistors and achieve a good relationship with everyone.

True Empathy

True empathy is seeing another person as part of a whole instead of a separate entity.

The more faith you have in Love, the more empathy you gain. True empathy is important in all your relationships.

◆ ◆ ◆

Grant Liberty

Always respect others. Do not insist on changing other people. Accept everyone as they are; flaws and virtues make us unique.

Liberty consists not only of keeping hands off, but also of keeping thoughts off.

Love Sets you Free

Since our infancy, we follow our parents, teachers and/or authority figures. That behavior is based on our survival, our need to be loved and avoid punishment. As an adult, you can review all those patterns freely.

Think rationally with Love and make all the necessary changes in your mind in order to lose the fear. You will become a mature, responsible and happy person.

From Conflict to Harmony

Fear is a sign of strain, which arises from a conflict in your mind.

Love exists. Fear does not. However, it is a powerful illusion that you have to overcome by thinking "union" instead of "separation."

Think, feel and experience only Love and fear will disappear from your life.

Cause of Fear

Fear is the normal consequence of seeing a meaningless world. Fear is the result of perceiving everything apart.

That idea of separation generates the beliefs in sin. Sin is an erroneous thought. We can define it as an absence of Love.

Where there is fear, there is no Love. You can eradicate the idea of sin from your mind by thinking with Love.

Every time you feel fear, it is because you are thinking without Love. Remember that what you see is the result of your thoughts. There is no exception to this fact.

The power of Love makes fear impossible.

Finding Happiness

Emotions come from the way you think. Fear can be controlled for a while, but for a life of happiness, you have to get rid of it. Instead of facing fear, people deny or project it.

Denial is not the Solution

Denial is a psychological mechanism that people use to avoid fear. When we are unable to tolerate a certain amount of pain in our minds, we prefer to think that nothing occurs. Like hiding the dirt under the carpet, denying is not a smart outcome. Face the situation with the certainty that Love is the answer to every problem.

Projection is not the Way

Another common behavior based on fear is to criticize, projecting bad feelings and blaming others. When we are unable to dissolve our guilt, we blame others in an attempt to get rid of it. Yet, blaming others simply reinforces guilt and increases fear.

The only way to terminate guilt is by thinking with Love and acting in consequence.

Giving or Asking for Love

The coin of Love has two faces. One side gives Love and the other one asks for it. Every interaction you have with a person is an opportunity to give this person Love, or to ask this person for Love.

Love is about giving. You can do it in many ways: when you greet someone, when you hug or kiss others, smiling, feeding someone, listening to someone who needed to talk, buying someone a special gift that you know that person wants, etc.

On the other side of the coin, there are many petitions of Love. Even though this may sound strange to you, when someone is threatening or attacking you, deep down, that person is scared and is asking for Love. Maybe you cannot give this person your Love because you are not ready to do so. If that occurs, take a breath and merely think something positive. It will be beneficial for both of you.

Replacing Fear

The recipe to eliminate fear is through right thinking, which is the same thing as expressing Love in your life.

True Love replaces fear.

Love is the alternative to thoughts of fear.

Dissolving Negative Feelings

Single thoughts of separation induce guilt. A mind that rejects Love can experience guilt.

Come back to your real Source! Dissolve your feelings of guilt by thinking with Love!

There is no fear or guilt in Love, for Love is fearless and guilt free.

More Pleasant Every Day

Think positive all the time and you will perceive a different world. Every day will be more pleasant than the day before.

The goal is being able to feel the energy of Love that keeps the Universe in motion.

World You Want to See

What you see outside is a pictorial represent-ation of your own thoughts.

Perceiving without Love creates disharmony and a vengeful world. You have to be determined to see things differently.

Remember that beyond your perception there is real Love.

Think with Love and discover harmony and peace beyond all.

Motto

What you think, you bring into your life!

The more you think with Love, the more you have the power to overcome problems and transcend conflicts.

Let the essence of our being "the Love you are" emerge from your soul, mind and body!

Understanding

When you ask for the understanding of your mind, receive inspiration and enlightenment, perfect loving thoughts come immediately.

How Does the Process Work?

Imagine you are inside a dark cave and want to get out. A remote light is not always the exit, but it allows you to follow it in order to find the exit. The same happens with your thoughts. A single positive thought is not the solution, but each thought can show you the way.

Thoughts of Love are steps you are walking down toward the road of Light.

Stop Judging Others

When people make a mistake or perform a negative action, you understand that this behavior is the consequence of their level of consciousness.

Do not judge people, not because you want to look nice, but simply because doing so will help you complete your healing process.

A Better Way

Judging others is exposing your own unresolved issues.

Thinking with Love means understanding and being compassionate towards people.

When you have worked long enough on yourself, you do not feel the need to attack or judge anyone.

Only One Lesson

You are Love, and Love is Perfection.

Any problem in our life shows an absence of Love, and a lack of forgiveness.

Forgiveness is the source of healing.

What is Healing?

Healing is a correction of the mind, and an actual integration of your mind, body and soul.

Path of Healing

If you align your mind with the Love within you (mental healing), you are able to heal your body (physical healing).

What is a Miracle?

A Miracle is a thought that you think with Love.

A miracle is a form of healing; it gives you strength, and leads to peace and tranquility.

Gift of Forgiveness

Forgiveness is a powerful tool you can use to release the past and live with joy in the present.

Forgiveness is thinking with Love.

A person who forgives is confident and radiates peace because forgiveness is a "conflict free" experience.

Imperfection is Gone

To forgive is to overlook. Look beyond error, and do not let your perception rest upon it.

By forgiving, you do not see imperfection of any kind in anybody, and you perceive that everything is fine.

True forgiveness is seeing people and life with new eyes and letting Love come out from your heart to solve problems.

Rituals

Rituals structure your mind in every way possible. They are positive, especially when you are a child; however, they are not necessary for forgiveness. It is up to you to ask for forgiveness.

If you prefer to pray or repeat a statement, this may help you shorten the process.

Living in the Present

Harboring resentments and criticizing keeps you stuck in the past. Remember that the past does not exist. Grievances hide to the world the Light that you are. Thinking with Love helps you walk more lightly in the present.

Learn from Your Mistakes

We all make mistakes because they are part of our learning process. Never criticize yourself under any circumstances. Instead:

1) Recognize the mistake, so you do not repeat it. Learn the lesson.

2) Ask for enlightenment to know what to do.

3) Move on!

Significant Understanding

Sometimes you consider yourself hurt by something that someone else did, and you feel like you will never be able to forgive him or her. Try to think loving thoughts about this person.

Knowing the person's personal history may help you to forgive. It does not mean that any conduct is justifiable. Just as there is a Heavenly justice according to the Universe's Plan, there is a human justice that keeps our civilization in order, allowing it to evolve. That lesson is also what that person has to experience and learn.

Forgiving starts with understanding.

Understanding brings appreciation and appreciation brings Love.

Appreciation

Appreciation is the only appropriate response to people.

You create the circumstances of your future life through your actions upon others.

Appreciation is a manifestation of Love.

Teaching by Example

You teach all the time, from the time you get up in the morning until you go to bed.

You teach when you greet others, with your speech, with your way of eating, with the way you are dressed, with your way of working and even driving. You are a teacher.

Nothing teaches more than example.

Others will watch and learn.

Your responsibility is always to behave toward reconciliation, integration, union and peace.

Teach only Love, for that is what you are.

Dealing with Difficult People

What about people who talk or behave in a negative way? What do you do?

People, who are fearful, often behave in a manner that creates unfortunate consequences. Frightened people can be vicious. All fear comes ultimately from the denial of Love.

First: Bless them with your thoughts.

Blessing someone does not mean that you cannot set a limit if necessary, or say no.

Second: Teach the right behavior by example.

Best Action

By opposing resistance to the other person's aggressive behavior, you reaffirm that both are wrong. The best action to take toward inappropriate behavior is to overlook it; setting your limit and being calm.

Time

Time is a learning device.

Just as a young child learns to walk, you need time to practice falling, banging and getting back up, until one day you acquire the ability to think with Love in any situation.

You need time to traverse your own journey. Take advantage of every minute of your life and acquire the ability to think loving thoughts.

Most Important Moment

Your mind has difficulty grasping the present, which is the only time that exists.

If you are not thinking in the present, it is because you are not thinking with Love. Thoughtless ideas preoccupy your mind and the truth is blocked.

Try to have many good moments in the present. In doing so, your experiences today will become your best memories tomorrow.

Live in the present! It is a matter of choice. It is an attitude and a selection of good thoughts.

Consciousness

Some people think life is a struggle; but it is not! Only our lack of consciousness of Love creates any struggle with living. Raise your consciousness by thinking with Love.

Learning from Experience

Whenever you have a problem, try to resolve it with Love. Ask yourself, "What do I have to learn from that experience?" If you get the message and you learn it, be sure that you passed the exam and that lesson is not going to repeat itself again.

Accept Yourself

Love yourself. If you made a mistake, forgive yourself. Every mistake is a call for Love. You did your best with the level of understanding and consciousness you had at that moment.

Loving yourself means healing yourself.

Any kind of healing involves replacing thoughts of fear with thoughts of Love.

Keep your mind full of loving thoughts.

Experience Builds your Future

Experience is important because it is how we learn. You can suggest that someone do or not do a certain thing; chances are that person will ignore your advice and act as they wish.

During our life nothing happens by chance, every event is hiding something we must learn. Only after living through an incident, usually harmful, are you able to change your behavior about something.

Positive experiences do not teach us because most of them invite us to stay in our "comfort zone" and nothing new arises from there.

Undesirably, only negative experiences (like an accident or an illness) shake us up, but at the same time give us the opportunity to discover the hidden message behind them.

Main Principle

The main principle is that there is only One Mind, One Source, The Divine Presence and Infinite Intelligence: Love.

At some point in our journey, we all must be able to love humankind and for each of us to feel the Unity that we are a part of.

Your goal is to connect with your real essence, "Love" by removing all the obstacles you have placed between you and others. The results will manifest in all your relationships.

Golden Rule

Remember that no one has the power to direct your life but you.

People live their lives according to their personality, preferences and the culture they belong to.

I propose that you live according to your heart, in line with the Golden Rule of Jesus:

"Behave towards others as you would have them behave towards you."

◆ ◆ ◆

Thoughts to Steer by

1.   There is a Major Plan.

2.   You are a Social Being.

3.   Same journey with different paths.

4.   Three groups of relationships.

5.   Motto.

6.   What is healing?

7.   Live in the Present.

8.   Teach by example.

9.   Accept yourself.

10.   The Golden Rule.